A New True Book

THE APACHE

By Patricia McKissack

CHILDRENS PRESS ®

CHICAGO

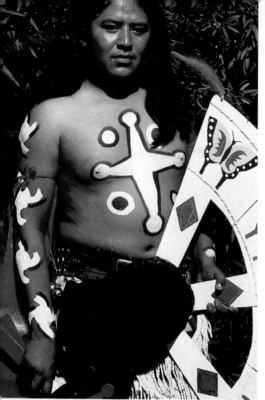

Apache man at modern
Native American celebration

PHOTO CREDITS

John Running— **cover** 2, 4 (top), 19, 35, 45 (left top & bottom)

Museum of New Mexico—10, 33 (right), 38 (center)

Henry A. Schmidt, 25 (right)

Edwin A. Bass, 6 (right)

Dana B. Chase, 15 (right)

Ben Wittick, 6 (left), 26 (bottom right), 36

J.R. Riddle, 24 (left)

William H. Simpson, 26 (top)

Arizona State Museum, University of Arizona, Tucson—11, 29 (right)

Walter Lubnek, 9; Helga Teiwes, 13 (right), 30, 31, 45 (right)

Reinhard Brucker—12, 13 (3 photos, top left, center, bottom left), 21 (right), 23 (right)

Lynn M. Stone—23 (left), 35 (2 photos)

Reproductions from the Arizona Historical Society—15 (left), 33 (left), 38 (left and right), 43

Courtesy of Special Collections, University of Arizona Library—17, 21 (left), 24 (right), 25 (left), 26 (bottom left), 29 (left), 41

Cover—Apache Devil Dancers

Library of Congress Cataloging in Publication Data

McKissack, Pat, 1944-
  The Apache.

  (A New true book)
  Includes index.
  Summary: Describes the history, customs, religion, government, homes, and day-to-day life of the Apache people of the Southwest.
    1. Apache Indians—Juvenile literature. [1. Apache Indians. 2. Indians of North America] I. Title.
E99.A6M43   1984   970.004'97   84-7803
ISBN 0-516-01925-2   AACR2

   11 12 13 14 15 16 17 18 19 R 02 01 00 99 98 97 96 95 94

TABLE OF CONTENTS

Apache girls model traditional clothes.

THE APACHU

The Hohokam, the Mogollon, and the Anasazi were early peoples who lived in the Southwest. Later, Pueblo peoples like the Zuni and the Hopi lived there.

Then hunters from Canada moved south in search of food. By the 1400s they claimed a share of the land that is now northern Mexico, Arizona, New Mexico, western

Bonito, a White Mountain Apache (left), and Chief San Juan and these Mescalero Apaches (right) were photographed about 1883.

Texas, and parts of Utah, Colorado, and Oklahoma.

The Zuni called these newcomers *Apachu*, "the enemy."

The Apache were not farmers or herdsmen. They were hunters and fighters.

THE APACHE GROUPS

The Apache called themselves *Tinde*, "the people."

The Apache nation was divided into six groups: the Navajo, Chiricahua, Lipan, Western Apache, Mescalero, and Jicarilla. (The Navajo later separated from the Apache. They became an independent nation.)

The Apache knew their kinsmen by the language they spoke and the way they lived. How the Apache did things and what they believed was called the life-way.

There were differences among the Apache groups. However, those that lived in the desert shared many of the same beliefs, as did groups that lived in the plains.

Apache wickiups could be moved easily.

Most Apache lived in small bands of five to ten families. They shared work and food. The bands moved when the animals they hunted moved or the seasons changed.

9

This Apache family camped near Roosevelt Lake in Arizona about 1918.

Each band had four or
more campgrounds where
it lived for three to six
months at a time. These
camps were near water
and were safe from
surprise attacks.

APACHE WOMEN AND MEN

Apache women built the
family huts called wickiups.
Women also gathered
twigs and brush to make

An abandoned wickiup

Apache *ramada*

their *ramada,* a shady
place for cooking, sewing,
and child care.

Women made the family
clothing. Animal skins were
used in early times. Later,
European cloth was used.

FLUTE

DECORATED POUCHES

CEREMONIAL DRUM
USED IN RITUAL DANCES

The pouches (left), flute (top), ceremonial drum (center),
and dolls (right) are examples of Apache craftsmanship and art.

Apache men were
hunters and fighters.

They spent long hours
making tools and weapons.

Apache men loved
storytelling. It was a
favorite pastime. They also
enjoyed games of running.

APACHE MARRIAGE, LAWS, AND CUSTOMS

When a man married,
he went to live with his
wife's band. He took care
of his wife, her parents,
and her younger sisters
and brothers. A man could
have several wives. But
he had to be able to
provide for all these
families.

Apache family (left). About 1890, another Apache family (right) was photographed bathing at Ojo Caliente, New Mexico.

There was little crime within the bands. An Apache who stole from his own group was a thief. A thief was made to give back the stolen goods and a bit more.

Anyone who killed a member of his or her band was taken to the victim's family. They passed sentence. Sometimes the sentence for murder was a beating; sometimes it was death. The worst punishment was being asked to leave the band. Living alone was unbearable for an Apache.

Geronimo (left, on horse), and Natchez (right, on horse), were famous Apache fighters.

APACHE LEADERS

Every band chose their own leader. He had to be strong. He could not brag.

A good leader listened to his people. He cared about them. He shared with them. No selfish person could ever be a leader.

At council meetings, local leaders sometimes chose a *nantan* as their spokesman. This is the closest thing to a tribal "chief" the Apache ever had. There never was a "chief" of all the Apache.

Apache
devil
dancers

RELIGIOUS BELIEFS

Ysun, the life-giver, was the Apache's most important spirit. Ysun sent the mountain spirits, called Gahns, to teach the Apache how to live. Ysun also sent White Painted

Woman and Child of the Water to help them.

Every year all the Apache honored their spirits. They danced special dances and ate special foods.

The di-yins had charms and powers. These people could cure the sick or tell the future. They could give advice. There was a di-yin for everything in the life-way—marriage, birth, hunting, war, and much, much more.

Apache medicine man (left)
and a hunting charm (right)

No Apache would go
near a burial ground. They
were afraid of ghosts.

No Apache ever spoke
the names of the dead.
Their ghosts might appear!

Property belonging to a
dead person was burned.
Otherwise the dead might
come back to get their
belongings.

Owls and bears were
believed to be forms used
by ghosts to hurt people.
So those animals were
feared, too. An owl feather
was thought to cause
sickness and even death.

Cochise Peak (above) is in the Chiricahua Mountains (left) in Arizona.

The number four was lucky. Doing things four times was a part of the Apache's everyday life. The four directions—north, south, east, and west—were important to the Apache, too.

Apache women carried their babies in cradle boards.

GROWING UP APACHE

Children were important.
After birth, a baby was put
in a cradle board. The
mother carried the baby
for at least six months.

Geronimo's son and his wife (left). In 1892 Desar (right) was the Apache scout for the Tenth Cavalry.

In the spring of his first year, an Apache boy was given his first haircut. His hair was cut three more times. Then it was not cut again. Some men had hair that reached their waists.

Hoop game (above) played by the White River Apache in 1901. Before
they had rifles, the Apache hunted with bows and arrows (below left).
They used them to fish in this 1885 photograph (below right).

The young Apache boy grew up listening to stories about hunting and raiding. Each boy knew that someday he would be a hunter and raider like his father and grandfathers.

Fathers made bows and arrows for their sons. The boys learned to hunt.

The boys grew older and stronger. Their fathers taught them more. Boys learned to run long distances. They were taught to use their senses—smell, touch, taste, sight, and hearing. Boys also learned how to move quickly but quietly.

As a boy neared his sixteenth birthday he was prepared for his manhood test. He had to go on four raids with the men of his group. If the boy did well on the four raids, he was called a man. He was free to marry, hunt, and raid with the men of his band.

He could even become a leader.

Apache girls were taught how to build the family's wickiup. They learned how to do things the Apache way. At about age thirteen

Apache women learned to build wickiups and to make strong, colorful baskets.

The past and the present meet, as visitors watch a young girl take part in an Apache ceremony.

every Apache girl was
given a four-day feast.

The girl was dressed in
white. A wickiup was built
for her so people could
visit and bring gifts. During
the four days the girl-
woman was believed to

The Apache keep their ancient tribal traditions alive in today's world.

have the powers of the
first mother on earth, White
Painted Woman. She could
give blessings and bring
good luck to her people.

After the ceremony was
over, she could marry. It
was the most important
event in a young girl's life.

GATHERING, HUNTING, AND RAIDING

The Apache got the things they needed in three ways: gathering, hunting, and raiding.

Women and children gathered food. Plants, fruits, and nuts were eaten.

A few bands grew corn, pumpkins, squash, melons, and chili peppers.

Apache on horseback (left) gather acorns in 1920. Corn (right) was an important food crop, too.

Every Apache male hunted. Deer was their favorite meat. The Apache hunted alone. First the Apache hunter greased his body with animal fat. This was done to cover up the "human" smell.

The hunter put on a mask made from a deer's head. Then he waited.

When the hunter killed a deer, everybody ate. The meat was shared with the whole camp.

Some animals were not eaten. Prairie dogs, snakes, turkeys, and fish were believed to be unclean. Otters, badgers, and mountain lions were hunted only for their skins.

Bald eagle

Eagles were trapped and two or three feathers were plucked. Then the birds were set free.

The Apache thought of raiding as another form of hunting. Settlers called it stealing, but the Apache didn't. To them it was necessary. They raided

Chiricahua Apache camp on the San Carlos River in Arizona about 1885.

ranches, small towns,
and wagon trains regularly.
They took what they
could use.

Raiding parties were
small—four to eight men.

APACHE WARS

For nearly three hundred years the word *Apache* meant "death" to Spaniards, Mexicans, and all settlers.

In war, the Apache gave no help to an enemy and asked for no help. They sometimes showed mercy to those who fought bravely, but cowards were killed in horrible ways.

Some of the greatest Apache fighters were

Mangas Coloradas (Red Sleeves), Cochise, Geronimo, and Victorio. Apache fighting men prepared themselves for battle. For four nights they did the "angry dance," or war dance.

Mangas Coloradas (left), Victorio (center), and Natchez, son of Cochise, were Apache fighters.

The men painted their faces and chests with the signs of war. They put on war caps made of hide. Then quietly they left camp. Their families waited. Apache men fought to the death.

The Spaniards were the first Europeans to explore the Southwest. The Apache began fighting them in the 1700s. When the Spaniards left in 1824 the Mexicans tried to defeat the Apache. They lost.

In 1846 the Mexicans lost Arizona and New Mexico to the United States. At first the Apache did not fight the American *Pindah*, "white eyes."

Settlers came to the Southwest. The cowardly acts of a few people ended the peace. The leaders, Mangas and Cochise, fought the Pindah with a fury. But Mangas was killed.

Cochise knew that his people could not beat the

General Cook (second from right) met with Geronimo (third from left).

soldiers (Blue Coats).
There were too many of
them.

Cochise tried to end the
wars. Then Cochise died.
The Apache were told lies.
Promises were broken. At
last they were forced to

leave their lands. They were made to live on reservations. It was a bitter time.

Victorio and Geronimo were two Apache leaders. They tried reservation life, but their people were miserable. So Victorio and Geronimo led two separate groups away from the reservation. The Blue Coats hunted them down.

Victorio was killed in Mexico. Geronimo was captured in September 1886.

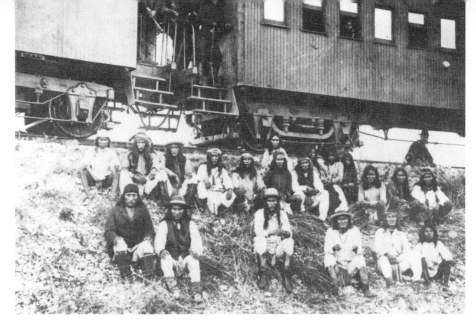

About 1886, a group of Apache, including Geronimo and Natchez, was sent under armed guard to Florida.

It took five thousand soldiers to force him to surrender. He was sent to Florida with many other Apache.

It was not until 1914 that the Apache were allowed to return to the Southwest to live.

THE APACHE TODAY

Today the Apache people live side by side with other Americans. Some Apache are farmers, others are cattle ranchers, journalists, filmmakers, teachers, and doctors.

The old ways are not gone. The Apache still do the dances and tell the stories of times past. But things have changed.

The Apache have a saying. For everything there

Apache lumbermen (top left), mothers (left) and grandmothers (above) live in the modern world, but they keep the old ways alive.

is a beginning. For all things there is a reason for being. When that reason is over, there is an ending... then a new beginning.

WORDS YOU SHOULD KNOW

band(BAND) — a group of families living together

belief(bee • LEEF) — something that is believed in, usually by a group of persons

brag(BRAG) — to talk about oneself boastfully

ceremony(SAIR • uh • mo • nee) — a formal ritual performed in a serious, established manner

charm(CHARM) — a word, phrase, or object that is believed to have magical powers to help or hurt

claim(KLAIM) — to take possession of as the rightful owner

council(KAUN • sill) — a group of leaders representing those who elected or named them

coward(KAU • erd) — one who is afraid and has no courage

explore(ek • SPLOAR) — to search in order to discover something

gathering(GATH • er • ing) — the collecting of plants to eat

independent(in • dee • PEN • dent) — separate; no longer part of a group

kinsmen(KINZ • men) — relatives; people joined together by something in common

leader(LEED • er) — a person who leads or directs a group

mercy(MER • see) — compassion or help given to someone who deserves punishment

miserable(MIZ • er • uh • bil) — unhappy; uncomfortable

newcomer(NOO • kuhm • er) — someone who has just arrived

pastime(PASS • tym) — something done to make the time pass pleasantly

Pueblo(PWEB • loh) — several groups of Native American farmers in the Southwest who live in permanent villages built of brick and stone

punishment(PUN • ish • ment) — a penalty given to a person who has committed some kind of wrongdoing

raid(RAYD) — to make a surprise attack on

reservation(rez • er • VAY • shun) — an area of land kept by a government for use by Native Americans

selfish(SELL • fish) — having excessive concern for oneself, without thinking of others

sentence(SENT • unz) — the punishment for a crime, as given by a judge or court

spokesman(SPOHKS • muhn) — a person who speaks for others as their representative

thief(THEEF) — one who steals

unbearable(un • BAIR • uh • bil) — not bearable; too terrible to be endured

unclean(un • KLEEN) — impure and not usable because of moral or spiritual beliefs

INDEX

About the Author

Patricia C. McKissack and her husband, Fredrick, are freelance writers, editors, and teachers of writing. They are the owners and operators of All-Writing Services, located in Clayton, Missouri. Ms. McKissack, an award-winning editor, published author, and experienced educator, has taught writing at several St. Louis colleges and universities, including Lindenwood College, the University of Missouri at St. Louis, and Forest Park Community College.

Since 1975, Ms. McKissack has published numerous magazine articles and stories for juvenile and adult readers. She has also conducted educational and editorial workshops throughout the country for a number of organizations, businesses, and universities.

Patricia McKissack is the mother of three teenage sons. They all live in a large remodeled inner-city home in St. Louis. Aside from writing, which she considers a hobby as well as a career, Ms. McKissack likes to take care of her many plants.